Five Little Monkeys

Five little monkeys swinging from a tree,
teasing Mr. Alligator, "Can't catch me."

Along came Mr. Alligator quiet as can be,
and snatched a monkey right out of that tree!

Four little monkeys swinging from a tree,
teasing Mr. Alligator, "Can't catch me."

Along came Mr. Alligator quiet as can be,
and snatched a monkey right out of that tree!

Three little monkeys swinging from a tree,
teasing Mr. Alligator, "Can't catch me."

Along came Mr. Alligator quiet as can be,
and snatched a monkey right out of that tree!

Two little monkeys swinging from a tree,
teasing Mr. Alligator, "Can't catch me."

Along came Mr. Alligator quiet as can be,
and snatched a monkey right out of that tree!

One little monkey swinging from a tree,
teasing Mr. Alligator, "Can't catch me."

Along came Mr. Alligator quiet as can be,
and snatched a monkey right out of that tree!